All the Colours Fade

For F.O.S. Rex regum, the value of your friendship has only increased with the gravity of years.

James Wilson

All the Colours Fade

The Hippocrene Society
Neverland Publishing
2012

All text and images © 2012 James Wilson,
except 'Dragonfly', p. 20, © 2012 Devon Pearse; and
'Tarka's Field' and 'Pityme Inn', p. 92, © 2012 Beryl
Wilson.

Book and cover design: James Wilson

All rights reserved, including the right of reproduction in
whole or in part in any form.

The Hippocrene Society
An imprint of Neverland Pubishing
2012

Printed in the United States of America

ISBN 13:
978-0-9826971-2-2

www.neverlandpublishing.com

CONTENTS

Adore!	1
Drummer	5
Cascade	9
Unstoppable	13
Au Revoir Monsieur Malin	17
Elizabeth	21
Sister	23
Motorway Of Stone	27
Shot Down, Not Out	33
Is This The One	37
The Resurrectionist	41
Shoeless	45

Play, Angels! Where?	47
Full Fathom Five	51
It's Coming Here	55
Gernika	59
Angels	63
Fools	67
The World Waits	71
Elephant 7	75
Thames Paradise	79
Pearl	81
Hanging Here	85
Elephant 12	89
Your Time Will Come	93
Boy On A Pedestal	97
Burning	101
Afterword	107

All the Colours Fade

'A chance to banish the memories of Turin.'
  B.D. 22.06.96

†

Adore!
***

It starts with a rendez-vous in the desert. He said he had an offer that was too good not to be heard. Arriving in a cloud of dust and a retinue that vanished into thin air, he was suddenly standing next to me in the wilderness, beaming an unholy smile. I listened, I always listen. I actually rather enjoyed his patter, the way the words rolled out of his mouth tripping into each other like dominoes, a cumulative effect of what I can only describe as grandiosity. Nothing stuck. Nothing sunk in... but I did admire the sounds, the cadences, the rhythms. It was impressive. I stepped out of myself and saw its seductiveness. I am only myself. But I am always stepping out. The two are not mutually exclusive states where I am concerned. I hadn't told him about this. I don't really think he wanted to know. I don't think he could know... he wouldn't understand. Or maybe he did understand, but faced with such futility in the event of that understanding, just preferred to feign ignorance so that he could still believe. Still cherish the dreams of opportunities. He swayed from side to side as he spoke and I could hear the music that he heard in his head... and it was good. Seductive, swaggering. Ambitious. But that was where his pitch fell flat. I'd heard it all before. I'd conceived everything he could ever possibly have to say. He talked about what I *could* be, what I *could* achieve if I let him on board. His appearance was so naïve I almost felt pity for him. (I did feel pity for him.) Adored? What did he know about being adored? Everything I have done (and I have done everything) is to be adored... also to be hated, spurned, desired, needed, worshipped, cursed, denied, affirmed... but above all to be adored. Anything but be alone. The way he spoke to me though, slick, slippery and smooth, I felt that he felt he could accomplish something, it was like he really thought he was talking to a fellow creation.

ADORE!

And so I fully immersed myself in my creation, my humanity, and I felt how vulnerable a man could be. I concentrated on my flesh, clenched and unclenched my fists, felt the blood rushing round my veins, the sun on my skin, the sand and salt encrusted in my matted hair and between my toes. I felt so alive and headstrong. I started to speak, a hushed cracked whisper as I got used to working my voice: 'I don't have to sell my soul. He's already in me.' He took a step backwards, slightly flustered, as if he hadn't expected me to speak, perhaps he hadn't even thought me capable of it. 'I don't need to sell my soul. He's already in me', I repeated, bolder this time, my voice finding its range. 'I wanna be adored' I whispered and then I spoke it, I bellowed, and my humanity left me as the refrain grew ever louder. 'You adore me', I gesticulated, 'You adore me.' And when I next looked around he had gone and the dust had settled and I knew that I could begin again.

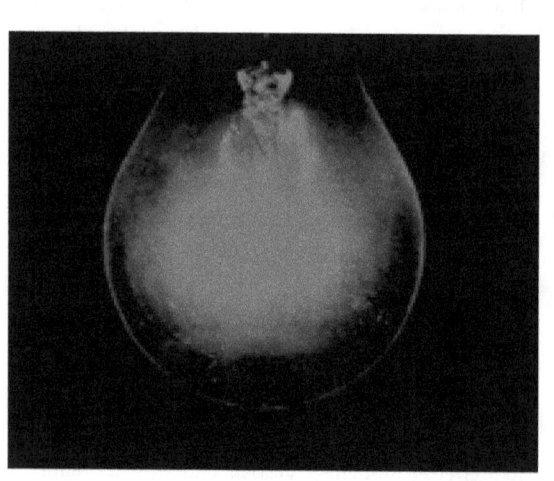

†

Drummer
***

In this sun-drenched, dust-filled border town where all we seem to do is hang around, it seems as though something's about to happen—I can feel the siesta slipping from my shoulders like a shawl. We're just leaning on lampposts, sitting on kerbsides, kicking cans like we do every day, but there's something in the air, I can feel the tingle in my belly too. Anticipation. I start to tap my toes, this no listless dissipation. Put my ear to the baking tarmac and I can hear the distant rumble reverberating. Is it wheels in motion or is it something more—I can hear a groove now, rhythms, beats and more. I'm so hungry for this and yet I feel strangely full. I want it. Where is it? Who is it? She's coming. Who is she? Where is she? Why is she? She's coming. Folk run in along the streets now, ever greater numbers. There's whistling and screaming and their faces are ecstatic. Presentiments of sentiments about to be born, we are the sheep soon to be shorn, someone's got something here to bestow now; it's nearly here and I'm good to go now. Primed. Alive. And here it is—a flotilla drawn by galley boys twelve as the ticker tape sidewinds down and the music smothers earth and sky, invading bones and tissues, making them twitch and bounce. The horns blow Jericho loud and the screams and shouts are just as deafening. Oh man, where did all these people come from with their bodies jostling and oppressive? Someone else's sweat is drying on my skin. And I'm almost beginning to care and then I see her. A Liberty waving, statuesque; a pageant-smiling face and a mile long dress, train and veil the colours of rainbows, like an old woman's parrot, a prism, a ghost. We're all just leaping now, molecules of boiling liquid turning to gas. This feeling's forever, but can never last. Eyes and smiles chime, glint like noonday glass. People fan their palm leaves, stoke up clouds of dust. The wave of noise is coming, bears down like a tidal bore.

DRUMMER

From out the hollering and klaxons, a rhythm starts to grip. Our jumping, pulsing movements lose no urgency, but something else is added, some kind of synchronicity. We sway and weave like leaves of grass upon the breeze. And here she comes now and she brings the melody. Stretch out our arms now, petals to the sun. The galley boys are straining in chains of dignity, and now the float is passing in slow-motion destiny. I can't tell the difference between anything, there's no distinction, I don't think it matters, we're all just tremulation. The shade of her, it passes, moves forever on, and we stumble out of kilter, but still dancing to her song.

†

Cascade
***

I stand outside the castle walls with my lantern on my back. My eyes survey the valleys, the flocks upon the hills. The fences, farm buildings and fields. All their different shades of crops. It all looks so peaceful, but how peaceful can surrender ever be? This place is tainted. A patchwork quilt of land just waiting to be pulled from beneath the unsuspecting feet. Bound to the whims and the vagaries of a man in a castle that no one has ever seen. I stand outside the walls. With my back to the castle I feel my strength begin to return. Far beyond the horizon, for several days or more, I hear the waves call me. I take a path. I walk across a moor. Sleep in a forest. The brooks goad me with their childish verse: 'go on water, floweth!' I always look forward, through marsh and peak and fen. Each new dawn brings birdsong and fresh hope. And with every stride I take towards the sea, I am loosening my yoke. But all the times my heels rise and fall back on the earth, remind that I'm not free yet, remind me of my worth. The fear is always there, like a hand above my shoulder. And I am flinching, waiting for the tap. I will not recognize the emissaries, if they are sent. But I will understand their words and the way they will link with both my arms and, in spite of my endeavours, they will turn me slowly round, drag me through the wheel ruts and the gutters of the streets, past every single footprint that I ever dared to tread, until I'm back inside the castle and its imaginary chains, plying my illusions to all those who know my name. With every hill I crest both hopes and fears mount. I will not look backwards no matter whose eyes bore into the back of my skull, no matter how fond the whispers in my ear. The labourers in the fields do not speak as I pass, but sometimes one will pause and lean against his spade or rest his arm upon the side of a cart. I cannot bear to ask how far I have to go. Each day I keep on walking, the

CASCADE

broadening river in my sight. In the towns I feel safer, and weary too at times. I think that I could stay there and hide for just a while. But the amnesty of namelessness could never last and soon I'd be a townsman with my lantern and my past. One day I reach a city and on its further side, in the suburbs with the refuse, I hear the gulls begin to cry. The mournful mewling spurs me on and I run beside the road, following the hauliers, laden with their loads. The river has widened to become an estuary and in the distance I see what might be freedom in the choppy choppy sea. I think that I hear sirens behind me, calling me back, or perhaps in pursuit. I run faster than I've ever run before. I stumble down the shingle and fall upon the shore. The sirens wail in the distance, but that might just be the wind. The salt air lashes my face. At the end of the breakwater, I step aboard the craft. Raise the sails, loose the moorings and soon I am adrift. Arrows rain down about me, the arrows of my name. But I mustn't turn around. My eyes water as I sail into the waves. Nothing in front of me, everything behind me. I have never felt so free of burden. The emptiness will fade, I'm sure, in time. And it must be advantageous, as I flee above the depths. I hang my lantern from the prow and look ho.

†

Unstoppable
***

We row and we row, making good progress over this lake that is a sea. I used to be a fisherman and I know how to handle an oar. I think of my father and his lack of protestation when we departed so suddenly. Has it been weeks, or months, or years? I've never had to flee for my life so many times. I've never felt so alive. I look up at the clouds racing past the night's purple mantle. The sky seems to be filled with more stars every time I see. And to my right, sharing the same plank as me, as we have done since our infancy, my brother, wearing that grimace of concentration and exertion as he heaves to the steady rhythm that beats within each one of us. All that we have experienced! It is wonderful to have someone beside me who has shared it all. The boredom in our home town, the endless routine. Sometimes I miss it. Sometimes I think we'd have been safer, more comfortable, richer perhaps, maybe we'd have found wives. The clouds are massing now. There is still time for all that. And I don't even need to look at the faces around me to know that I could never be safer than with this crew. But what have we left behind! The stars still blink as the cloud bank shifts and sunders. Then suddenly the thunder rolls out like a roof above our heads. The sea that is a lake is still. The rain patters down. Wheel-scattered gravel sounds. And it's like we're in one big room, a hall, a vaulted dome, sitting on the mead-benches, will we never feel the cold? The rain drops splash like kisses, a film upon our skin. Our muscles and sinews strain at the oars, invigorated. Onwards we row. Lightning flash. Eyes narrow, grimaces of attrition. The storm is fierce, the rain heavier and bruising. And yet the lake that is a sea is still. We make no progress through its waters. Neither shore gets nearer, nor more far away. The waves now crash around us, but don't break upon our hull. We draw in the oars. 'Can

UNSTOPPABLE

we sit this one out?' our unsure expressions seem to ask. No one wants to break the silence. And it is silent. The rain's gone out like a light. Hands clasped between thighs. Like resting. But not. Where did this mist come from? It surrounds our boat like an army, like a shield wall. It bears down on all sides, coaxing out tiredness. In all my seafaring years I have never felt how flimsy is the barque that holds us from beneath. The waves are starting up again, buffeting us from side to side. Maybe they never stopped. Maybe nothing ever stops and sometimes you just forget. There is a cold wind whistling in our ears, the sound of barren eternity. Breakers break, rollers roll; we slide down the benches and shoulders press shoulders. We fall from our seats. Sodden knees. Mumbling? Is someone mumbling? My lips are trembling. Is it me? An audible gasp. What now. A luminescence, another vessel 'pon these waters? A figure through the mist. A human figure through this mist. 'Don't stop, isn't it funny how you shine'. He says to us, voicing our awe. He steps on board, laughing, making fun of our fear. We are relieved. We're thick as thieves. Lower oars and proceed. Get the rhythm back, get up to speed. Another memory pasted on the palimpsest. It's too much; sometimes nothing fades away completely. Everything is perpetually returning and at times I don't know where I am. That meal we shared in the tavern. The bluesman playing his guitar. Lying with my back to the fire. Sleeping under the open sky. People coming and going. Reconvening: coming back to a state of harmony that keeps somehow getting disrupted. Was it all one time? Is there any distinction? Those crowd scenes. All those crowd scenes. So many faces. Falling through me like beams, too much for the rods and cones to process. Leave me reeling and nauseous. Need to latch on to the constant. That man? We hauled him up from the deep. No, it's the other way round. He stepped aboard. Where did he come from? When was this? Oh, that was now. He must be one of us. I open my eyes and the night soothes like a balm. The stars are many and fresh; but this lake that was a sea is not still enough to bear reflections; and we row and we row.

†

Au Revoir Monsieur Malin
***

Helicopters circle overhead. I remember last year when the persistent chirruping was the cicadas. Some say they spend their summers indolently, singing all the live long day. And when austerity arrives, they fear for their lives, and have nothing left to say. We promised we would never make the same mistake. We will never run out of words. We will never drain our well of songs. But just let me think back a little while longer, just let me enjoy this sun. Shield my eyes with the crook of my arm, let me linger before I'm done. Damn these drones. Repeatedly cutting into my daydreams with such insistence. But with the grass cool against my nape, I'll defer for just five minutes' reminiscence. Unfurl my proboscis for another hit of nectar. Let the sap rise, trap me in the amber of nostalgia. For some reason, it's always motion imagery. Sculling boats, cycles, arms out of windows on the passenger side. The flicker flicker of shadows. The trees that were beacons flash by. A hangman's oak. Cedars of lebanon—spectral silhouettes (no matter where the sun might shine). Lombardy poplars lining the roads for a never-ending cavalcade. Thank you for your appreciation. But now it seems that the forests we entered have been left as deserts in our wake. Time to cut down the cutters? The blades above stoke up the air. Surveillance to check resistance. How naïve. We may be basking (stalks of corn hang from our mouths), but we're just heating up our blood. Residues of reptilian brains. The sense of smell is the oldest sense and I smell trouble. Our pride will stretch its legs and soon we will be sated. Blooded maws will stream rosettes on our lapels. The stirring starts. Time to rise, flow from the parks and the gardens, turn the faubourgs inside out. If I could see what they could see from their horseflies in the sky, I'd be worried. I'd expect the tail to swish. The populace is coursing and won't be dammed.

AU REVOIR MONSIEUR MALIN

Their barricades close the streets, but open the way. They come with armour and batons. We just come to sing our songs. All around we're dervish hopping, as the chorus breaks from our hearts. It swells and emanates about us, the whole is like its parts. The surge is inevitable. They raise sticks, we raise hell. They try to fumigate us, but who is the real pest? They'd like to kill this, but who is already dead? Is it a paradox: the more of us they try to divide, the more of us there are to divide. Hydra-headed, it can't be said that no one flocked to our side. Projectiles fly and multiply in looping arcs of triumph. Keep singing. Don't draw breath to cheer, don't use your hands to applaud. Everything is possible. Long live the ephemeral! The whole world is a spectacle! It's just our vision that is flawed.

†

Elizabeth
***

I have been standing on street corners and in the back rooms of bars. I have been sitting in underpasses, and alcoves, or between the pillars of a marble colonnade. And wherever I have been, people have passed. And wherever I have been, people have heard. I am not prescient and I do not document. I am the something in the water. Part of the current. I am the troubadour of trouble, a balladeer of boiling rages. I have rung out like the chimes of the town hall clock. I am the background sound that gets inside and festers. Lyre, fiddle, guitar or mandolin—the strings on the instrument may change, but the tune remains the same. They have heard my song and levelled, they have dissented, quaked and shook. They have charted situations upon which I was compelled to look. I saw before what for, and I saw some guy. The communes swarmed around me many a July. Sometimes I wonder if I'm blessed or if I'm cursed. For everything I see will someday soon be reversed. I always see the truth and I always see the aim, even though many years later when I play the same refrain the truth has become a falsehood and a receptacle of blame. The last chord of my song fades into the air for whose sake? And yet again I'm left lamenting: the beast that is awake.

†

Sister
***

I sit bolt upright when I wake—I've got that sinking feeling in my heart again; am I falling or is it just another mistake? I can never be sure. I get dressed and make for the door. Outside it's so much earlier than my average weekend. Empty streets, birdsong, cool sunshine and I think I'm on the mend. Getting back to usual. Is that good, though? A few nights later and I dream. *We're running. Broad boulevards. Crowds part and reform like a red sea, our pursuers caught in the swell. Thwarted. You've got blonde hair. But I can see your roots. You smile. Laughing, relieved. It's no palace, but it'll do. Dark and grey and sepia. Dust dancing, unable to settle, shaken by rhythm we can't hear in this silence. You stand by the window. Will we ever catch our breath? Feels like—hold on—pause... wait just... there, doesn't it feel like love? We both start laughing. Love only ever feels like moments. I surge forward, leave the sofa seated. I don't know, but I panic. There it is: a noise. We're being invaded. No rest for us now and here we go again. They come through the back. We're already out the front and gone. Let your guard down. Never let your guard down. But guards fall down like autumn leaves. We're all so seasonal in all we do. We run like siblings. Never seen you before tonight. Trust's instinctual. We'll die together before we betray the strangers that we are. Burst. Sun's out. Blue days, green days, we know it's lazy days now. Tree-lined avenues. Big green canopies. Lawns and grass and pollen. Holidays and happiness. We walk towards the sound of the river. Reeds and weeping willows shed the tears we no longer need. Hand in hand like paperchain children. I can't remember ever feeling threatened, this serenity's like a drug. There's a mix-up somewhere and I'm alone. I'm missing something, I'm missing someone. I know it, but I can't feel it. Or maybe I feel it, but I don't know it. I'm strolling along the bank alone, like I've never been otherwise.* I sit bolt upright when I wake and for the rest of the week

SISTER

I've got a thirst I cannot slake. I half-dial the number for the umpteenth time. Bad idea, good idea, I just can't decide. Indecision gets the better of me and the decision fades away. I persist in the comfort of my empty everyday. But a Friday night comes round and my friends have a request. Can we go to that place we went before. And of course I acquiesce. (Maybe it was my idea and I put it in their minds—I've had a few jars and I wouldn't be surprised.) Well, fancy meeting you here, and other pleasantries. I guess I'll see you later, but there are no certainties. I sit bolt upright when I wake to the sound of my door being gently closed. I've got that sinking feeling, but then I guess I should've known.

†

Motorway Of Stone
***

He emerges from the darkness on the far side of the bridge exhaling smoke. He walks with purpose. Clicks his fingers, clocks me without recognition. His percussive levity belies his granite face. He stops five yards from where I stand. And, as if he has hit a mark, he unfurls a grand sweeping gesture, indicating the flow of cars below. It is the action of a showman, the flourishing touch of a conjuror. I fear he has disappeared many things in the past and my stomach switches back on to spin cycle. *'The automobile'*, he says, *'... and the open road ...'*. That voice. Like someone's turning a crank and the words are dropping out in clusters, like coins from a penny-pushing slot machine. Is he announcing the title of some performance piece? He just leaves the words there, letting the cold night air slowly close back in around them. I return my gaze to the motorway, the garlands of irregular red and white lights, distorted by the persistent drizzle and the droop of my heavy-lidded eyes. Small ferns of spray are thrown up by every set of wheels. Winged-heels. It is so cold and lonely here. I saw no one on my way. All the houses, the windows, the drawn curtains, the parked cars, the dustbins full of evidence. Evidence of existences held in suspension. All the dreams have seeped from under doors and through cracks in the mortar to make this inevitable nightmare materialize. He has lured me into the liminal with nothing more than a location, a time and my own sense of perdition. The masterstroke of his manipulation was, I now see, in setting this finale against such a pulsing backdrop. Each aureola of oncoming diminishing light, each velcro doppler wave: a shell containing a kernel, a gob of cuckoo's spit. They are lives full of longing, maybe even empathy. But they are out of reach. Hermetic beings. Illuminations in the margins serving only to render the text of my story more black and white. Continual but unpredictable wakes of hope to increase the pitch of my screams. He is a big fan of dichotomy. 'You can't have the good without the bad', he once said, the words tumbling out between his onslaught of pauses. 'I let people be good'. He never lied to me. At the very start, he warned, with all due ceremony: 'Trying to stay ahead of the game is difficult. Trying to quit the game impossible. There's only ever one way out.' I guess that's why I've turned up. It's time to quit. He is starting up again, creaking back into action after a thousand cars have passed. '... *A symbol of independence; taking your life in your own hands. Empowerment! Freedom of movement! ...*' His gloved hand slips inside his greatcoat. I grip the balustrade and close my eyes. Am I praying? Am I wishing? Why is resignation never permanent? '... *But is it all just an illusion? A fevered fantasy? One more layer of boxes to trap us in. ...*' I screw my eyes tighter shut and grip the rail harder, my body and soul are folding in on themselves, white under the pressure of my unvocalized plea. Something gives and friction screams. The screeching is contagious. There are impact sounds and horns slammed incandescently. I let go my petrified hold. My eyes open on a cacophony. The car that tried to avoid his body is upturned in flames upon the verge; another car has spun perpendicular to the perforated lane divisions and been smashed into by a third. Dragged by a rear wheel, his mangled body blends in decorously with the tyre burns, hissing carburettors and shards from the windshield. The molluscs are emerging from their shells to reveal their dazed and bloodied fragility. I don't make appeal to their longing, or their warmth or empathy. I am the phoenix. I love the scene.

†

Shot Down, Not Out
***

It took them a while to find a viable candidate. I bounce the ball twice and serve. The way she moves from side to side on her baseline. I don't stand a chance. She's a permanent distraction and she knows it. I am in thrall. Later, in the pavilion (the players' lounge, no less), as we recline on deep-set sofas and pass around a spliff, I make it more than obvious how utterly besotted I am. She props herself up on one elbow, reaches down for the ashtray and, looking me firmly in the face as she extinguishes the joint, tells me how she'd love to do it and she knows I've always had it coming. I think she then formed her fingers into a pistol and fired between my eyes. I don't know if it was an imaginary bullet or an imaginary blank. She looked over her shoulder as she was exiting the room. I tried to get up and follow, but she slammed the door shut. Things were already a bit hazy, but I think I was happy. The circuit seemed to narrow after that and I began to see her everywhere. Every time I won and punched the air I would see her in the crowd or on the next-door court, shaking her head in disdain. Sometimes we passed in corridors and she would almost spit the words 'criss-cross' at me. Her venom only seemed to fuel my flames. Ok, I'll be the first to admit there were quite a few of the old guard who didn't like the number of fans I was winning... but at the same time, *I was winning fans*. There just seemed to be more and more of them at each tour and exhibition. The funny thing is, they didn't seem to care that much about the game; their attention was always much more focused afterwards, when I doled out soundbites and quips. I did know about waxing and waning. I knew I couldn't remain everyone's darling. And I knew the traditionalists were muttering more concertedly after each successive triumph. Yes, I knew all this. I even suspected savagery. For this reason, I found her background presence reassuring.

SHOT DOWN, NOT OUT

If the exposé was inevitable, I was glad it was going to be her. I've always admired beauty and there was something in her elusive and antagonistic attitude that made her even more appealing. I had to be shot down and I was glad it was going to be her. So it was no surprise when she came into my hotel room past midnight, unannounced. And it was no surprise that she kissed me tenderly. It was no surprise that with the same mouth she went and told her tales. And it was no surprise how things ended. But so little in life is final. I've regrouped, I might start training again, I might even think about making a comeback.

†

Is The One
***

The flocks of starlings wheel around the twilight sky. The dipping rising movements are hypnotic and dizzying, an otherworldly spectacle that only seems to further emphasize the abandoned nature of the town beneath. From my vantage point on the moors, the grids of housing and streets are almost indistinguishable from the fields of rubble and polluted waterways in which they rest. I put my finger to my lips and in one fell swoop the birds fall to roost on the window ledges and warehouse eaves. The augury leaves me none the wiser. I still await confirmation. I don't want to see the town's lights grow stronger. No sodium glow for me. I've got to believe that place is empty. I am the other kind of émigré. The cold wind plays about my untucked shirt—I am very poorly dressed for any kind of adventure; but in every other way I am well prepared! (I've got to believe.) I can get no signal here so I jump and start to run. Back to the lay-by that she selected from the maps she carried in her head. The car is still there, parked in a predetermined direction. I've had dark moments before and much of my past seems to have been spent walking in the constrained spaces on the narrow side of the lampposts, with barely room enough to manoeuvre without stumbling into the gutter. But just recently I've started to flex my legs. None of this limbering was my idea. I'm sure I've always been a follower. I've left just enough tension in my newly liberated limbs to give us the spring we need from these blocks. I can't countenance using it to pedal backwards, to prostrate myself before I've even had a crack at the prodigal. Where can she be? I don't like the way these doubts are creeping in; it only ever happens when she is not with me. I thought she was consumed by the same desire. I didn't even think when I was in her presence... I knew. How can such certainty seem to be floundering on the cusp

IS THIS THE ONE

of the great escape? I murmur the mantra we made to keep up our morale: Burn the town, burn the town, burn the town where we were born. It sounds rather hollow without her beside me. The words are devoid of the promise they once contained. But I can't go back. I get in the car and wind the windows down. I strap myself in and turn on the ignition. As I release the handbrake and the car rolls slowly into motion, the chill breath of the oncoming night makes my face shudder.

†

The Resurrectionist
***

I pound my gavel on the lectern, because I'm sure I serve more than one court. I look below me at you faces in the pews. I give you literacy and I give you news: I am the resurrection! You won't understand it. You might believe it, millenarian jackals that you are, but you won't understand it. I wanna be elected; I am selected; I am elected. You? hmmph! I pace the pulpit like a caged tiger and the more I prowl and the more I growl the more you'll howl, I'm sure. I've hammered and I've slammed my theses in the door. Just to give you a sense. But you're poor because you're poor. I'll let you run with it. I'll let you run riot with it. Build up a whole head of steam. Then I'll step aside, say not justified, and let you all get skimmed like cream. Wasters. What's a massacre in the face of salvation? Some reformation! Book learned, the heads I've turned, you come running at my beck and call. I champion the masses, bring them back out the morasses and yet I hate them all. I prefer the company of princes (if they toe my line), because they can grant me wishes and save my fat behind. Like that time: in the forest. I don't think I realized just how much I'd put my head on the block. I thought I was the untouchable hero. It came as quite a shock. I was suddenly dependent on the hospitality, guidance, and promised taciturnity of others. No looking down from that position. Gave rise to the question: just who the fuck did I think had given me the right to claim to be some leading light radiating privileged insight? Whose spokesman did I think I was? Just another icon waiting to be smashed. I didn't even hold the reins to the horse that I was riding. I was being safely conducted into hiding. Yeah, I had some doubts. Wending our way through the evergreen trees that screened me, but also obscured the view, my thoughts played on what I'd done and what I planned to do. Nothing peaceful would come of this, my heart did seem to sigh; power corrupts all systems, it's just the way, so let it lie. But the fire in the belly kindled and my pride was sparked with ire. Take me to the castle, then, and hide me in some tower. Just give me books and pens and inks and I'll still glower my glower. And just look what I achieved! I changed the course of history. At what price, some might say, but such pipsqueaks and dumb squealings are rarely worth my time of day. Sometimes I do think back to that forest path and I seem to see it full of gorse and briars; lightning flashing overhead, and the pine trees set on fire; I feel like I'm getting trapped and lost and the brambles creep up higher; they bind me tight and tear my flesh as the flames get ever nigher. But at other times from all about, I just hear choirs singing, and through the trees I see emerge the bright light of a clearing. But these, I'm sure, are just the dreams of a man who made a difference. A man who stood up to all with a given grace and no undue resilience. Oh these wheels I've set in motion; these lines that I have cast. Let's call it a devotion, and hope the buck will soon be passed.

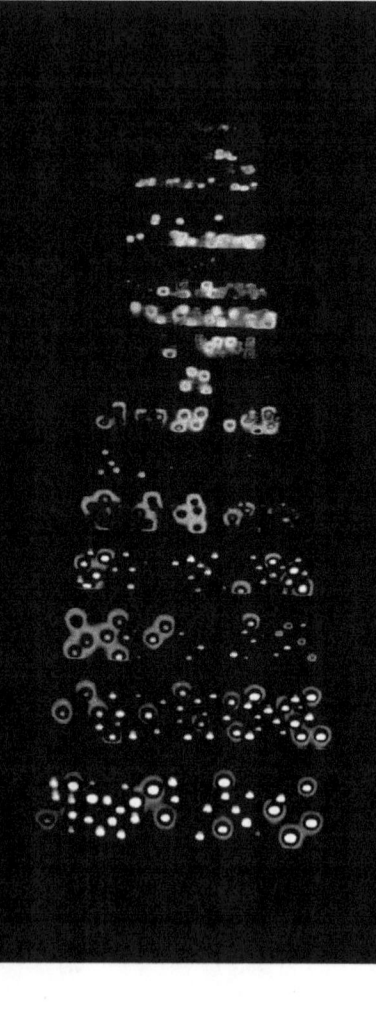

†

Shoeless
***

They well up from nine fathoms deep, but there is no distance here; they stream up from the abyss, burning green and white and blue. They are supplicants, they are not artificial. They will bear all they have to bear. They have put off their externals. They are plastick and innumerable. Foxglove wrapped in foxglove. Hear them please. I am just a guest here. I kiss their naked feet. I can do nothing. The features of their faces are forever changing—everyone I have ever known; no one I could recognize—a composite of all their number, rendering the countenance moonish plain, yet not devoid of expression. Too much expression. Too much pain. I feel pity for all mankind. When can I go home? There is too much emotion here for me to ever understand. These multitudes rise up around me with each step I take—what am I trampling underfoot?—and just as soon as they arrive to let out their entreaty, they are gone again, telescoping back in on themselves, returning to be dinned in tuns and gyres. I'd turn in my shoes, but these latchets will not loosen.

†

Play, Angels! Where?
***

Our progress is slow, the camels are heavily laden. They are noble, stinking beasts who know all too well the inclemency of men. We left at midnight. It had to be under cover of darkness. We had assurances of the temporary blindness of the authorities. Diverted by the blood and lust of self-prophesying orgies. It's not that there are spies everywhere. Who is there left to spy for? It had long since become a regime of overt persecution. And one was made a target simply for not joining in. The desert sky is seamed with stars. It is so cold at night. The heat evaporates so quickly from the ground. I am loath to return to the nomadic life of before. I have a family now. We are making for the mountains, a slow and gradual climb, and we will follow them to the sea where there is believed to be a town where tolerance is still permitted. As we reach the incline and my horse picks its way between the rocks and the esparto, I question for the first time the heaviness in my heart. Should not the shackles be peeling, melting with relief? I am surrounded by those whom I hold dear. We are the lucky few. We are escaping. But as much as that word contains a goal of freedom, it has at the root of its head a moving out of, a moving away from. Out of bonds of degradation? Away from tyranny? Yes. But that preposition *from* is unshakeable once it attaches. It is a tiny little hook that won't let go. My wife, my daughters, they are from there. I am from there too. I wandered for many years, mistaken in my belief that I could pace that word away. I followed the spice route; caravanserais of slaves; I sailed on clippers and whalers. If I could make the acquaintance of everywhere and anywhere, then I would have no need of somewhere in particular. Or so I thought. But I grew tired and returned, learning only after fifteen years of exile (self-imposed), that there was no scythe strong enough to cut off my roots. We

PLAY, ANGELS! WHERE?

wind our way alongside the wadi and reach the mountain peaks. We have been travelling for nearly three hours now. We should be far enough away. There is a roar overhead. It is hard to tell where it is coming from as it echoes and rebounds between these hills and those opposite. It is terrifying. There are piercing unhuman shrieks as roseate and aquamarine lights stream above. The blast shoves me against the pommel of my saddle and my horse buckles to its knees. I think I can feel the heat; the orange glow of the conflagration is reflected back off the escarpment above us and all around. My wife is looking over her shoulder crying salt tears at the sight. That used to be a home there.

†

Full Fathom Five
✳✳✳

I bubble up pockets of sea; pinch them; splash them like puddles; throw them in the humans' faces like an affront. It's a front. I'm not really this playful. I've been unlucky. Earthbound and down. Stumbling from spell to spell. Trapped into toadying, corralled into a kowtow. Sometimes I yearn for my cloven pine. I take a spin around the island and in an instant I am back. It's pointless really, but sometimes it gives me a sense of release. Tend to the tempest, just another pan upon the hob. I'm a plate-spinner and I care not for the crockery. They mean nothing to me. Will I never get the chance to work through my grievances? I feel the longer they are neglected, the more irrevocable they become. How now, Moody? My master doesn't know the half of it. I used to be somebody, once. My memories, though, are gone. Sometimes a question pierces through the fog and retrieves an image from the past and I feel a little confused and embarrassed as though I've just been unexpectedly sick. Time too seems to have faded clean away. I see it happening to the herebelows, but it never grants me grace. I just fluctuate in my see-saw states of sycophancy and resentment. I wreathe people in love and sleep and scheming. It doesn't feel like deceiving. My morals are vacant. They were set hard and fast in years past and now I can't recall them. I don't think it matters too much, for I comprehend so little of what I do. He talks about his art. He gives me less credit than an inkwell or a horsehair brush. It's still more credit than I want. I am a tool and a toy. I do what I'm told. But that leaves me mindful of my muse—for if I now narrate, who knows the news? I sometimes fear that there is a master behind my master. And who knows what behind that! Lined up like pylons. Looking glasses reflected in looking glasses. It leaves one wondering. I spin around the island and in an instant I am back. More larking about with melody and apparel. Tabors and tabards through dingle and dell. Leading and luring to some conclusion I won't understand. No release. There always seems to be one more task to hand.

†

It's Coming Here
***

The galloping thrum of horses' hooves is being drowned out by a chasing pack of white manes. The waves are relentless in pursuit, swallowing all the land in their path with a simplicity that is staggering. Much of the town is already submerged, the surface broken here and there by roofs rendered lily pads and towers and steeples poking out like piles in some perfidious pond. The saint races on ahead, occasionally throwing accusatory looks over his shoulder. The frenzied roarers behind are sending out forerunners, and spray is thrown and hissed up in my face. The strong hands around my waist are not there from affection, but desperation. The grip is less paternal than a lifeless pinching shut of iron tongs or tweezers. Did I expect anything else? There were times when my father, momentarily weary from ceaseless sessions of debauchery, would stumble into my rooms, perhaps attracted or repulsed by the quietude and cleanliness. He would look at me with those glazed-over eyes, struggling to recognize who I was, then murmur, 'Oh, it's you'. I wondered if I detected disappointment or regret in those few words: that he couldn't annul me with the violent deaths he accorded all the other women, the myriads of mistresses who were lured or taken night after night from a seemingly never diminishing stock of naïve nubiles prepared to overlook all precedents for the chance of being crowned queen. A chance so slight it's a wonder anyone could ever see it. But they did… and they held on to it to the exclusion of all else. The alternating cries of ecstasy and agony radiated out from my father's quarters into every last reach of this once great walled city of ours, saturating the citizens in a contagious lust that ripped up every restraint in its path. The saint turns around once more and shouts at me impatiently to 'Release his hold!' This is the wrath of God and the waters will not wane

IT'S COMING HERE

till they have smothered the source of sin, covered the cause of corruption. Kill the king. Orphan his daughter. The saint slows and lets us draw level. He starts to whip my father about his face and across his back; trying not to catch me, but, infuriated by this additional hindrance, lashing out all the wilder. My father's grip weakens and, amidst his animal grunts of pain, he emits a plea for help. The saint had shared with me the warning voice he heard in the night. An all too accurate forecast of the divine vengeance he had so long craved. But looking at him now, his face contorted with rage as he raises his whip again and again with unremitting authority, I see something colder than the sea. I shake my feet free of the stirrups and the harness slips through my hands as I am pulled backwards.

†

Gernika
***

These confined spaces have opened up new ways of thinking. To no one's benefit, I fear. The manufactured intelligence put paid to my colleagues... and I put paid to it. In our training they told us to prepare for no return. Even if plans went as projected they had no way of knowing whether the earth's atmosphere would embrace or burn up our homecoming hulk. We said we understood. We accepted the terms. We didn't believe a word. It seemed impossible to imagine anything but success. How frail were we! Alone now, far beyond radio contact, somewhere in the outer reaches of the empyrean, I have only the ghosts of my past for company. They taunt me with their attainability. I am the ultimate passenger. Coasting to an end that can't come too soon. Coasting to an end that I won't even recognize. Indistinguishable from all the spectra I am sailing through; passages of light caused by speed and distance or just malfunctions of spent synapses? I am aging so rapidly. Yet I can't free myself from the suspicion that it is not I that is growing old and being extinguished, but all else. I long for my wife and child so much that sometimes I am with them. But I am always the third person looking on, an alien presence incapable of getting the feelings right. It only hurts me more. But even that pain is numbness. When can I stop being the spectator? This torture is uncalled for. The pressure grows more and more intense until it focuses with unparalleled precision. I awake in a set-piece salon. Paintings drip from their frames. I can hear the fragile bridge of my breathing, so far away it seems to come from another dimension. This is artifice. Beautiful artifice. Where can it have come from, if not me? The floor is made of light, the furnishings come from centuries past, but are fitting. Sparse and surgical, but the colours bring celestial reassurance. I see myself. I am myself. A lonely meal for one—the

GERNIKA

emptiness amplified by the splendour. I see myself. I am myself. Decrepit, bedridden and woebegone. A black gown of finality. I see myself. I am myself. I understand now. It was all so simple. I reach out to the void and feel newborn.

†

Angels
***

If you should always start at the end, as a schoolday critic once maintained, then, I guess, we drift off in utter bliss, sun's warmth on closed eyelids, and the giving weight of entwined limbs. But we shouldn't neglect beginnings, the stories wouldn't be worth the telling without them. Primal, those who came after would call it... with envy and a certain degradation typical of their knowledge. This place was a vestige of verdure, an eruption of evanescence from the bleaks and wants that went before and crept in so soon after. Your eyes couldn't cope with the colours. That's not some boastful jibe, no lapsarian lament. It's just a futile attempt to describe what these words can't quite describe. Fail me! Of course it can't be so, but it's the way that I recall; we were grounded, yes we were, but my God, how we soared! Vales of wonder, we read the landscape with our hearts. And when contentment brimmed over, the scenery tore apart. Constant renewal of what we already felt reflected in the shifting surroundings. I had one to share it with. You knew it too! We had more in common than anyone hoped we'd realize. But we realized. And it wasn't like all the colours faded, but more like we just came in bloom. We needed each other more and more and everything else began to seem irrelevant. Unqualified imperatives entered our instincts and insatiability slid in with no relent. Oh this desire! How it needed to be expressed! So she took me by the hand and we hatched a plan, knowing we'd be seen. Down we went to the dappled shade, where the sun's rays were oblique. Against the trunk of a trusty tree, we determined on a scene. We articulated first in verbals, but the meaning was incomplete; so, we articulated with our bodies, from our lips down to our feet. The camera seems to pan out from there, retreating ever back and upwards, out from the restful bodies, away from the watchful tree, leave

ANGELS

the dale unfolding in green and blue and green. And I guess that was the ending; the beginning too, it seems. I'm not sure it matters, undistinguished from a dream. A milestone, perhaps, a measuring post, in deed. How far we came, how far we've gone, if all can be believed.

†

fools
***

We used to be a posse; when the Sierra Madre made some sense. Now there's been a rupture, this expanse only serves to emphasize the cruelty and conniving. There's no hiding. No denying. We have turned on each other. I don't trust not damn one of them. Not as far as I can throw them. We saw a glimmer in the desert. Now the only things that glint are the knives we clasp and the barrels of our guns. We flash them about like fool's gold, constantly provoking one another to make a decisive move. We used to share stories—they made the way shorter and less barbed. Now we only share malice and bared teeth. The only pleasure comes from torment which we drink in deep long draughts. How we laughed! At those we left behind us who said we were chasing spectres. We'd show them. We were a team, we kept alive the dream. And then it broke. I don't think any of us could pinpoint it exactly. But I remember one morning, waking up round the embers of the fire and resenting their haggard unkempt faces. Why do we all sleep with bags under our heads at night? What have we got to hide? I thought we said we were all in this together. The constant lack of finds as we reconvened at the end of each day's digs seemed suspicious. Who suggested this? One of us; and another had a map; I had the horses; and the fourth with the sack. We were foils, a team, an egg. Now look at us! Now look at me! We're the dregs we ran away from, the scum that had to cease. And if no one's got the goods to give, then there'll be no release. The horrible thing—and it's something that I fear the most—is that we thrive in these conditions. An autocatalytic cataclysm. We can't wait to see the end of one, 'cause it will bring the end of all. End it all. Is that hope or despair? I don't know. But it's one of the only redeeming features we've got left... and yet, when we manage to brave

FOOLS

out the morning bile and spit out the cuss words from the day before, we saddle up, cool as fuck, and hit the groove just as before. And I know as I look about us, jaws chewing on matchstick splints, that we have something unbeatable within us. And were one to perish, that would vanish. And that's the worst crime. I think they know it too. That's why every time a blade is pulled, or some other weapon brandished, it's eventually put aside. But when we separate, as prearranged, shovels on our shoulders, we toil alone and hope to own what we find beneath these boulders. That's where the trouble starts and ends. We wind on through the hills, wind on for fifteen days or more. We saw the falls that promised all. But when we came back from panning, there was only three. And it gave. It all gave in. We melted. Couldn't bear no more accusations of treachery. Some of us soldiered on, but our hearts weren't really in it. And in the end the time was ripe, the time was ripe to bin it. We tossed in all our gear, the bags we held so tight. We set them all afire, we set them all alight. What a sight. The flames flared large and bold, and as we walked away in different directions, our shadows grew ever longer ahead of us. They loomed and bobbed and reminded each and every one of us that we knew how to strut.

†

The World Waits
***

Click shut locks and wind back clocks. Spend the last of your currency tonight. An empty pocket won't weigh you down when you take one of your next flights. Laissez-faire or let's make do? A sunset attitude. Spin this globe beneath your feet and never let the darkness rise. (There was enough of that within to induce from those without the sigh of sighs.) How to keep everyone in sight whilst remaining well hid—it's not so easy without regime machinery. So stay on the move. Scuttle from island resort to mountain retreat. Try to pull in favours from the ones you didn't beat. Present yourself as... a gentile Ahasuerus who no longer wants to cause a fuss. Just in need of a constant getaway. Anything that will bide your time is surely worth a try. A stay of execution till you can raise your boot's heel high. And crunch their impudent wing casings into the dirt. A nation's treasures once bought you leisures. Now they buy the distance to keep you from the hurt. Your facial hair looks too hastily grown. You dress like a beggar. But nothing can hide your tan of privilege. An image that once stood proud, now stoops not to conquer, but to survive. How you survived! Clinging to power like a parasite. A blood-engorged mite. A life-sapping blight. Do you ever close your eyes and think about how such disparate and numerous peoples have been brought together by the shared fantasy of seeing you swing by your feet from a lamppost, a haunch of rotting meat? No, of course you don't. You're just waiting for the love to return. You can flog a whole lot of love from a little whip of fear, if you wield it right. Do you feel the fires blazing at your back? Mansions marauded, compounds cracked open... and laughed at! The vanity of tyranny reveals itself in even the smallest of monogrammed details. Yeah, you know it. You don't know it. You're the blindest sightseer. I hope you always have to look over your

THE WORLD WAITS

shoulder. I hope you never feel at home. I hope that in your wanderings you always feel alone. A silhouette of nothing diminishing into dipping sun and waning day. You don't even have the dignity to turn and watch your empires fade away.

†

Elephant 7
***

I am a barker. I love that little word. The carousel goes spinning round. Isn't life absurd? I've had the pick of the lookers. I count them all as tips. I leave everyone unsteady with my merry-go-round of quips. For all my carefree reeling, my ne'er-do-well's bow-legged stance, I can't help this feeling that I'm tiring of this dance. It only takes a small crack in my abrasive veneer to give somebody some hope that they might not have to fear. All of a sudden I'm snared by one who's timid and who's plain; but she was there when I needed care, so I guess I can't complain. I lounge like a lizard, I bleed her slowly dry. Her depths of devotion—enough to make one sigh. Sometimes I weary of her always being so right. I lash out, no excuse, I'm a sorry waste of spite. The robber comes a calling and I'm lured into his scheme. The money's unimportant; but it's a chance to vent some spleen. Instead I end up mooning about birds sitting on the wire and all the trains that have passed me by—such nebulous desire! Of course it all goes wrong, how could it ever have gone right? I'm left lying, she's left crying, he slips into the night. Burst into heaven; time to ride on those toy trains; I'm surrounded by suicides, such miseries and pains. I'm a charmer, no self-harmer, I deserve another day! Down through the heavens, no time to enjoy the cotton clouds. I'm booked on the red express: ten years, no appeals allowed. Time elapses and I emerge a broken man of dubious reform. I'm the one in a million, but this experiment seems thoughtfully ill born. To get my heart's desire I am granted another day; but I can't get through with tricks and treats and am told to go away. My temper's not been tempered, as a man I have not grown; the slap rings out like an elephant stone and I leave them all alone. The memories are better, even if they're sad; they've no use for the likes of me—but what a handsome lad! Back to the toy trains, back to

ELEPHANT 7

the cotton clouds, back to the holes in my dreams,
such ragged tattered shrouds.

†

Thames Paradise
✳✳✳

Downriver. I think that's the place for me. Washed out or washed up amongst the shells of vanished industry. Floating along on promises of renovation ever more renewed. Because as long as you make pledges, you never have to do... right? Perma-suspension of (un)delivery punctuated by occasional ribbon cutting. Faux revelry. But river splashed cash wets white elephant flanks and sooner or later everything has been developed into newbuild flats. Everywhere looks the same in the future. Everything diluted out to meet never-stated ambitions of conformity. There's a big F in future and they are perfecting it now: the laptop dreamers, the CGI schemers, the Powerpoint preeners. Chivvied by legacy cravers for backhand favours. Guarantee your name in alliterative epithets for popular modes of conveyance and hope that the affection will rub off. 'I eat over 40 tonnes of rubbish a year', the river claims via a placarded caption. The psychological detritus dumped daily is, however, incalculable. I'm beginning to feel that this society is getting a little too big for me. I head downriver, but it's a vanished sanctuary. Even the estuary is being claimed by the fantasies of floppy-haired buffoons. Build an artificial island for your flight paths to solipsism and runways to species-tainting arrogance. The waters will rise and cover these ego-driven scratches. Downriver will prevail. And my despair will surely drown.

†

Pearl
***

An out of season esplanade. The Christmas lights still glare. It's New Year's Eve, they're all inside. I take off for some air. Try to loose the fug, but it swathes my thoughts and deeds. Take the steps down to the beach and walk down to the sea. How many kind words have been said tonight? Is that just not our way? But if there's nothing beneath those playful masks, then there's nothing. Wolves in wolves' clothing. I'm freezing in that company. Perhaps I need to be colder to know the warmth I have. I used to be a strong swimmer. The morbid regularity and insistence of the waves, linking every shore on earth, a metronome for pithy existence. A judge-penitent once heard the sound of a body striking the water in the darkness. Afterwards the silence was unending. He did nothing. This black speck swims out to sea to become the unfading cry. The bells ring solemnly on the buoys. I must strike out further. Where are my friends? Someone once said that the sea is a symbol of worldly knowledge—what a way to drown! Grasping at nothing you can keep. All you once prized filling your lungs and dragging you deep. Reveries disperse. I briefly stoop to trail my fingers in the surf. I hunch my shoulders and pull the collar up on my coat. I head back to the tavern, pausing twice to knock some of the sand off my shoes. I am greeted with enthusiasm; smiles and embraces. Perhaps I've been mistaken. These are my friends. Get them in! I get them in. Long may this night continue. You got them in? I'll get them in. Now, get this one down you! Bind me with seaweed, soak me with dark brine. I'm drowning here and I'll drown for all of time. The lifebelts that are thrown in consist mainly of holes; I just keep on slipping through and cannot get a hold. Sometimes when I go under, I can still hear the voices up above and they sound like nothing I can cling to, nothing I can love. There are thousands of us threshing, being dragged beneath the tides; why do you, stowed safely in the boats, toss out so few lines? Leave us be now—it's no use. We cannot sink, we cannot swim and we refuse to choose.

†

𝔥anging 𝔥ere
***

The posters were strapped to the trunks of trees down where the road divides the forest's edge from the fields. Those fields filled with standing stones: menhirs plotted in patterns impossible to work out; a petrified crowd of people heading to and from some big attraction. What better setting to stage the circus? They draped the dolmens with fairy lights; flaring cauldrons on pedestals picked out a path through the families of megaliths; and across the night sky, the arc lights announced the arena in the distance. I remember the elephants' fanfare as we paid for our tickets—two beautifully marbled cards bearing just one word: *Bienvenue*. Men in candy-stripe jackets and red leather breeches bowed deeply as we passed. I shivered slightly with excitement; you put your arm round my waist. I remember the jugglers, lion tamers and stilts walkers; the human cannonballs, high divers and fire-eaters. My eyes widened at every turn, but none more so than when they stole a glance of you. All about was contentment and wow and I wondered whether it was for real or just some projection of the love tumbling and somersaulting out my heart. I wish it was. The blue and yellow big top beckoned; we took our seats in the stalls. A flash of strobe and a roll of drums and the show began. They swung through the air with such daring and grace. Leaps of faith and flights of fancy. He hung upside down with such ease and caught her every time, as though it were no more difficult than taking a book down from a shelf. I felt keenly how transfixed you were and heard the words involuntarily escape your lips: 'I could feel safe for ever in those arms'. After the act was over and the artists had returned to ground, shining like higher beings stooping to the levels of mere mortals, you asked to borrow a pen and ran down to the hoardings. You waited patiently and laughed as he wrote something more than his name down on your card. More than all that I remember the next day, as we walked along the sandy path through the woods to the dunes. We turned a corner and the wind that had been tousling the treetops died suddenly and you lowered your voice in respect, for the encroaching silence or my feelings, I'm not sure which. You let me down gently and with delicacy, concluding our own too brief trapeze act. The memory always fades at this point and I am slowly siphoned out the scene; hoisted reluctantly away to wherever the present may now be. When I returned to my homeland I did so harbouring your memory deep within me, for safekeeping. Hidden, put aside. But knowing all too well that its potent toxicity might seep out and enter the groundwater swell of my being. I never ran away to join the circus, such impulsive ideas could benefit me little. Instead I took classes, trained every day, diligently overcame my natural awkwardness, and, years later, auditioned for an entertainments manager who was impressed enough to take me on. I was ascetic and austere and, in time, commanded the craft. I have been partnered with great beauties, bodies lithe and supple. I have performed in tents on village greens to handfuls of disinterested children hungry for clowns. And I have performed in the most famous theatres all across this minuscule globe, to rapt expressions and necks craned with awe. Capital city or the back of beyond, I always take time to look out at the audience, even when suspended from my beam. You'll be a woman now, of course. In many ways I hope never to see your face. I prefer to return to that memory; an ache, but not necessarily of pain; just a fading resonance of the heights my heart was once capable of feeling. That sandy path, the flip-flop scuffle and being siphoned out the scene; indefinitely suspended; yearning to hold you in my arms.

†

Elephant 12
***

Halcyon. Halcyon. Halcyon! How specific can one go? The walk from the bungalow past the Polo-snuffling horses. Tarka and Daisy. The names don't escape me (though so much else has fled). Across the fields of gold spun into inviting ricks and stacks. Then, from a sunscape so bright it would blind your older eyes, disappear into the woods and a brindled light so soft you could stroke it. Everything that is green is resonant. Life pouring in through senses that are just so willing! Babble away my brookish friend, your lilting tones have gilded ears for years. And here am I, still listening so long after. Heed the call. Cross the wooden footbridge and wind on through the trees. Tickle the flanks of the stream with willow wands; cast in furry catkins and watch them race away. Ratchet up the rays with nature's subtleties. Sparser foliage and breaks in tree canopies. Feel the dust grow finer and more golden between your toes. Then burst back into the sunscape; walk through the caravan park. Feel the sea breeze and hear the amniotic echo of waves. Cross the bay-bound road and jump on the day-baked sand. Oh the tenderness of stone! My georgics and bucolics eat me up inside. This place; that walk; they cannot be found on maps. A golf course now, some say. And who am I to disagree? It's been years since I've been near the fable, or the locality. And the photos, the slides—if they exist, maybe in the third draw down on the dresser (developed by Truprint)—are not true prints, but somewhat faulty guides. And my moth-eaten memories? The holes in my dreams? Well, maybe somewhere in the cotton clouds they are stored in tact, preserved like unborn rain, waiting for the faithful recollection that will see them fall. And until then I should be happy enough flashing up the flaws and sifting through the ragged remnants. Such mind dust persists in being a representation of

ELEPHANT 12

what I am. So please don't pity me. You're probably not so different, the boundaries of your past being constantly waxed and polished until one day you too will realize that you haven't been left with shelves lined with distinct and radiant scenes; instead you too have somehow buffed all into a mass of blurred and semi-porous skins. So let's give the tombola another spin. Every ticket wins a prize! Slide the stylus back to find another place and time. Maybe I'll just end up where I was before—I don't mind, it's somewhere I have yet to find myself ever feeling bored. It hooks me in and I'm back walking through those fields where the combine harvesters have been busy reaping in and shaping up their yields. From the sunshine to the shade and here we go again, through the woods to the caravan park... Not different. Not the same.

†

Your Time Will Come
***

In the spirit of adventure I push aside the bracken and crawl through to the other side. Someone has tweaked the cyan levels here. Crotchets, minims and semibreves float out the bills of fluttering birds and burst upon my face. Ping. Pop. Plash. Am I waking from or walking into some kind of sleeping spell? Why haven't I asked this question before? Stumble down a bank, ease into a run. No exertion. An excursion. Drawn by I don't know. Stage set scenery, pulleyed past or through me, felt-tip coloured tropes. A distant castle in a darkened forest never fades from view.

ALL THE COLOURS FADE

The hint's not neon-arrowed, but clear all the same: prepare for end-of-level bosses and treat it like a game. I might have one more life left. So use an icon for a sword and watch the bramble clear; focus on the focus and let the path appear. Vault moats and scale crenellations; achievements nullified by dawning realizations: everyone who has ever been has done this before you. And the afterthought: that changes not a jot nor a tittle. Importance undiminished, significance still gleaming like gem-encrusted finery. Extract the universal from the personal; funnel the all inside you. It's a two-way street. (And probably a yellow brick road.) Once inside the battlements (that don't ask for that kind of fight), I float down spiral staircases, endless worn stone flights. Corkscrewing vertiginously, could this be an aim or exit in itself? A vague sensation of being concurrently elsewhere precipitates a massive rush—an unseen grab back and hurtle through the conscious undertow. Did someone call my name? 'Stop it!' Bright lights and people peering down at me. And then thrown back with a crash and a clatter and a running out of steps. A door painted in the wall breaks my newborn fall. Corridors lure me. I know what I'm looking for. I have always held the image of the soft and golden light of her chambers.

YOUR TIME WILL COME

And now I'm finally there. Tiptoeing redundantly round her bed. I am the vernal warmth that will raise her from her slumbers. I place the kiss on her lips. She wakes and the undertow removes me from the stirring scene, the longest of longshore drifts beaching me in another groggy time and place. 'You didn't like that one, did you?' is how someone greets my return, shining a penlight in my eyes and writing something on a chart.

†

Boy On A pedestal
***

That statue unnerves me. I resent the way the girls flock about his feet. They drape themselves about him in unbecoming ways. Fawning almost. Wasting affections that should be spent on us. On me. They say I need to relax a little. They shush me and shoo me away. But I've heard the stories. I've heard sounds at night. The only known work of a sculptor who dabbled a little too deep in sciences unspecified (but much speculated upon). It's also said that he dabbled a little too freely with other men's wives. He was put to death for one of these pursuits. I really don't know which.

But asked for some final words he is alleged to have come up with a curse. A sadistic grin smeared across his face, he promised that satisfaction is one thing the women would never get from the men of this town. He raised his finger as though about to say something else, but the hangman dropped the floor—much to the annoyance of the large crowd of female watchers. Some of the ladies looked a bit coy and hid behind the handkerchiefs they had raised to their eyes. So it goes. Just stories, the other guys say, trying to hold expressions of unconcern and complete self-assurance. But they know it. They worry, I'm sure of it. I'm not the only one walking around this town with a hangdog shuffle. Nearly every man looks broken under some burden (if you scrutinize him long enough). I blame that statue. Stationed in the centre of the square, there's nary a day you can spare from passing his smug and knowing features. Arm ambiguously aloft, with one finger outstretched. Greeting? Gloating? Beckoning? Warning? I abhor him. Such a weedy-looking youth. The girls all say he's beautiful and we should be proud to have him here. They have each invented stories about who he is: a poet, a peacemaker, a prince, an apothecary, depending on who you ask. But always a worrying amount of detail, usually

BOY ON A PEDESTAL

concluded with a sigh. Sometimes I wonder if they talk or think about anything else. They say I should stop asking questions then. More than once, in the half-light of dawn or dusk, I have seen him move. Well, maybe not move... but certainly with a guilty air about him, as though he has just hopped back on his pedestal, as though he has just recovered his repose. One of those times I thought I saw my ex-girlfriend running away down a cobbled side street. I have since started dreaming about ways to cut him down: with a pickaxe or a buzz saw and an enthusiastic crowd. Or I loop a cord about his neck and attach it to my car, rev the engine real loud then hit the pedal hard. Or I take some tools and hack and chop and hew and club and saw; I file and sand and fire and scratch and scrape and smash and claw. Or I go down empty-handed and butt and punch and kick. I pull and push and knee and chin—yet nothing seems to do him in. I wake up from the last one covered in bruises, shouting and screaming in the middle of the town square. And he just stands there unmoved and pointing. I follow the direction of his raised arm knowing well in advance that it leads to the bridge out of town and the river's inviting surge.

†

Burning
***

Put-put-put-put, our tails serve as propellers as we swim above the seabed, stealthily focused. Oh yeah, we are legion, and we're heading to the shores. When we land we hope to get our limbs back. We've got a mission. We've got lessons to lead. So softly spoken. How can such hushed tones be harbingers? Well, listen! You've had your chance. Now's mine. Ours! We have spawned and multiplied in absentia. Look how fat and lifeless you have become. Your inertia knows no bounds. This is going to be easy. From the dawn of time until this time that's mine, you've had it oh so uncomplicated.

But you've only really prospered to the degree that your appetites have been sated. But even then you weren't placated, developing ever more intricate ways of destruction. Tear each other's throats out; chain each other in cells. With a need to invent an enemy, you turned on your selves. But now we've returned from the primeval soup and sludge and look how quickly we're evolving. We shed our serpentine skins on the sands and now look at us—we're better dressed and more dignified than you. We may have cast off our tails, but there are remnants of a smoky seductive rattle. Your womenfolk can't get enough of our suave sophistication and your menfolk project all sorts of fantasies and longing on to a perceived sensuality. The couplings only harm one side and let's just say: we're still standing. You love the way we talk because we know just what you want to hear. We feel no pangs about spouting inaccuracy and displaying dissimulation, we learned it from watching you. There's a certain pluck and courage in adversity that we've always admired about you people; but it arrives just too late—vigilance and tolerance should come before resistance. You band together and temporarily suspend the infighting and squabbles. But the web is spun. We are so intricately threaded amongst you that you barely know who

BURNING

to lash out at. This tickled us. Bring in a regime of such taut manipulation. Allow no leeway and weed us out. Do you think you can spot us in the way we walk? Perhaps a certain aged cruelty behind the eyes? Or a curve in our figure? We are shapeshifters. You see us in anyone you want to. And the slaughter and purges begin. It's amazing how little we have to do. You damn yourselves so easily. So little persuasion required. All from your own accord and misguided determination. Your orators rally your remaining numbers, claiming the victory to be in sight, and we continue to stand amongst you cheering just as vociferously. Behind closed doors your bravado disappears and we hear the laments and unsunk fears. You refer to us as the plague. Some of the self-righteous amongst you call us a scourge and seem almost ecstatic with every diminishing population census. They are the worst of you. We will leave them to last. They keep themselves to themselves and become inbred from suspicion. They cage themselves behind fences and turrets and arm themselves to the teeth. All things come to pass. They look on with envy at the world outside. How effortless and tempting we make things appear. They compare this with their self-imposed rationing and weakening gene pools. They tear down their compounds from raw lust and within weeks the deed is done. You are gone.

AFTERWORD

I have lived with the songs of The Stone Roses for, in many cases, nearly twenty years, and they have become treasured friends of whom I have never grown tired. This collection of pieces attempts to exhibit the personal palimpsest the songs have become for me. I wanted to respond to my relationship with both the lyrics and the imagery of the music. Memories and dreams have combined with stories and scenes from literature, theology, film and art. Some of these influences have obvious ties to the songs, for example, the biblical imagery or the Shakespeare reference in the title of 'Full Fathom Five'. Other influences have come, at times unexpectedly, almost unwittingly, from writers and artists I have loved or lived in parallel to the timeframe of my intimacy with the back catalogue of the Roses: Kafka, Camus, Coleridge, Swedenborg, Kubrick, Yeats, Sebald, Sinclair, Maupassant and Borzage all flash past or linger at one point or another. The pieces were written whilst listening to the music of The Stone Roses—usually different versions of the song in question on repeat play. Sometimes a degree of free association or automatic writing initiated the process; sometimes I started writing bringing a backlog of images before I began. In either case formless fancies were honed, however minimally, into a semblance of narrative. For this reason—in spite of a frequency of rhyme, alliteration and other poetic staples—the pieces have been set as prose; but also because in this format the reader can pick up or discard rhythms far more freely than the setting of verse allows. The pieces are deliberately vague, with characters only referred to by pronouns, hoping to leave an openness to interpretation that might come somewhere near to the same ambiguity found in the inspirational lyrics of John Squire and Ian Brown. I hope (but don't necessarily expect)

AFTERWORD

that this will also allow the writing to stand alone and outside of any knowledge of The Stone Roses.

It remains for me to thank my parents, Rick and Beryl Wilson, for, in general, everything, but, more specifically, for letting me rifle through their photo albums. I would like to thank Donna and Joe Font at Neverland Publishing for all their work (and trust!). Thanks also to Ian Brinton, Anders Hallengren and Oliver Smiddy for their encouragement and for looking over early drafts. I owe a huge debt of gratitude to Devon Pearse, for her much appreciated support and guidance and her patience in reading through the typescript of these texts. Finally, of course, thank you to Ian, John, Reni and Mani whose songs remain constant delights and inspirations.

JW, September, 2011

James Wilson is the author of *Images of the Afterlife in Cinema* (London: Duchy of Lambeth, 2011). He is the translator of two volumes of the French writer Guy de Maupassant: *To the Sun* and *The Foreign Soul & The Angelus*. His prose fiction has appeared in the journal *The Use of English*. He lives in London.

www.ingramcontent.com/pod-product-compliance
Lightning Source LLC
Chambersburg PA
CBHW061331040426
42444CB00011B/2869